Moments In Time

Octavia Maufas

BookLeaf Publishing

India | USA | UK

Presentation by *BookLeaf Publishing*

Web: www.bookleafpub.com

E-mail: info@bookleafpub.com

ISBN: 9789358311877

First edition 2023

*To all the kids I've met that hadn't found
their voice yet. This is for you!*

ACKNOWLEDGEMENT

I would like to acknowledge the kind Psychiatrist, who once said, " You don't need medication, all you need is a journal and a pen"

PREFACE

Writing is therapeutic, but what happens when your journal entries turn into poetry?... Lets find out.

Silent Realms

It's foggy right now in the realms of my brain,
it gets so hard that the stress doesn't help me
maintain.
Im trying hard to explain, but I think that if I do,
my words would only be in vain.
I love the stormy clouds and the grey skies that
draw the rain.
When they start to fall, that is when I think
okay.
And to anyone out there, whoever you might be,
Please study me hard and tell me what you see.
Because I'm forced with all my might, through
the turmoil and despite, the fact that my heart is
like fresh soil.
So whatever the seeds may be that need to be
planted.
Whatever they are these emotions that are
matted.
Like nappy roots that form on your scalp,
This mess is irritating without a doubt.
Ill wash, condition, grease you and even comb
them out.
But we all know that every yank and pull ends
with a shout.
This is painful, it hurts!

This irritation gets worse!
With the minutes days hours and years,
I live with these things, I live with my fears.
So if I seem to not be able to explain with my words,
just listen to the tears.

Anticipation

I love you, I love what you say.
I respect you and I admire you in every way.
You help me to stay strong in your own special way.
Ive missed you, I miss the things you say.
I dream of you and your the one for whom I pray.
You modify the sun, you modify my stars and moon.
You are my nighttime, my daytime and you are my noon.
I know that I'll see you again if it's later or soon.
So to whomever is concerned or to whomever whom.

The Other Side

When people see me, they see a girl who is
happy and never cries.
But if they only knew me, the real me that I
hide..
Only if they knew whats behind the facial lies.
The expressions that i show make people glad,
but behind the reflections their very sad.
Like the saying goes, "if thoughts could kill"
These thoughts I have would make he Pope ill.
Thoughts of murder and death
tears of sorrow and painful regrets.
But these thoughts I have hurt me far much more
than I can explain.
Far much more even past the human brain.
You have to search deep down inside the pit of
loss,
Everything is my way I'm the * Boss!
So remember when you look at me, its not what
it seems.
Deep down inside I can be very mean.
So if you piss me off once I'll treat you like my
dreams.
I'll smoke you like a blunt and ill bind you to
your knees.
To me your the nightmares I have.

Not good always bad.
Your my excuse to stay up at night.
Thinking of you gives me fright.
Especially waking up in the middle of the night,
my face soaked with sweat,
tears dripping from my eyes onto my chest.
The memories are so bad, that when I awake I'm
never mad.
It's just the urgent jerk to sit up without my
regular scream!
So am I still to you, what at first I had seemed?

Blooming

I'm a flower, I'm just so poetic.
The way I rap, my style is very floetic.
And what I've said to you I don't regret it.
Because the thought of holding it in, my mouth
wouldn't let it.
If your asking who did it, Ill say he said it. And
if you wanna go there, then on your last pair of
dirty drawers I'd bet it.
But moving on to the bigger picture.
The subject at hand couldn't beg to differ.
Because I do like you and sometimes I hate your
guts.
And if you Mess with me, my foot will be up
your nuts.
So just go back to that Ashtray of yours &
pickup the butts,
now shove them in your mouth and inhale the
filthy sluts
of nicotine and the poisonous carbonide
chlorine.
Cough and choke while you spit up your lungs.
Now stare up at the ceiling like you've just been
hung.
While you talk about the love who has you
sprung,

Start talking about the pain that you will
overcome.
Now what I'm saying is very true.
I don't mean to hurt you I'm keeping it real with
you!
Because I wish you weren't so angry and in so
much pain.
I wish you still were able to say the things you
need to say.
I'll answer your questions and tell you what you
want to hear.
And the things I say to you,
are for you the things I fear.
Since your far away you might be happy where
you are.
I still wish you were near and not so very far.
When I look into your eyes and stare into the
gaze.
I no longer know who you are,
I only see the inner maze.
Just know that this obstacle in your life is
nothing but a faze,
And observe yourself when it's over, you will be
amazed

Wisdom

Wisdom is a gift of life.
This will shield you through turmoil and strife.
Using this tool wisely will gain you everlasting
life.
And his word is yours in an undertone, day and
night.
If it's wrong look towards the right.
When there is darkness just look for the light.
When in danger just call with all your might.
And wait longingly your reward will come by
flight.
Just keep faith with you, it'll be alright.
See right now I'm hurting, I'm scarred from all
your lies.
My body is in so much pain that my heart
literally cries.
Everyday someone dies,
and with every wind a bird flies.
Every mountain has to be climbed,
Every leader leaves someone behind.
The fig tree grows, the leaves grow tender.
In subjection to something comes a heartfelt
surrender.
In every victim there is an offender.
In a service sacredness has to be rendered.

When you regret something turn into a forgiver.
The hate shrinks small and your love grows
bigger.
Thank you for listening, whoever you might be.
Just say, "okay" and when your finished, check
back with me.

2003

Where is the love? is the question that is being
asked.
But where is your motivation when your support
is turning slaxed?
Aids is the main epidemic when your coughing
and don't remember there's anthrax.
When it comes to the prejudice, your opinion is
first,
But what about the facts!?
And then I think of children and their diminutive
frame of mind,
and how their often forgotten and left behind.
At night time I lay in the dark and stare at the
shadows on the wall.
And if the room door is cracked, I'm listening to
the sounds down the hall.
I open the blinds and look out the window.
I stare at the pavement on the street.
A car passes by and then I remember that their
watching me.
They know what I do.
They see how I act.
The read my appearance from the front to the
back.
And my body s like a revolving wheel,

with every sort of personal feeling that you
could ever feel.
I'm filled with double standards.
I still remember the hurtful slanders.
I'm looked upon as a vassal.
And I'm stuck most of the time with others and
their hassle.
Like giving a definition of the word chaos:
"The original disorder of formless matter and
darkness".
It may be to you, but the truth to me is harmless.
And with your heart, guard it with a harness.
Meditate on it more or less.
I'm just stuck with distress and I'm stressed day
by day.
More and more there is drama headed my way.
Now just remember to use your inner pinion.
And pay no ind to others and their opinion.
Regardless if on an accident you offend them.
Because in the end you cant turn to them.

Longing Part 1

Hey, how are you doing?
I'm doing fine.
I miss feeling your comfort and seeing you all
the time.
I still remember what you said.
I still have reflections in my mind.
Embroidered in my head.
Even though we're in 2 separate places,
I still wish we were together instead.
I miss you, what are you thinking? How do you
feel?
Do you miss me, do you care still?
When that day comes, I can't wait until.
Life is always an up and down kind of hill.
I appreciate you.
I am grateful for all that you do.
And with you, is where my heart feels so true.
Please tell me, please talk to me.
If i wrote you, will you write back to me?
If you found my number, would you call me?
Just let me know.
I really need to know.
If I'm alone to find out,
My heart would just be filled with doubts.

Longing Part 2

I pray like Luther,
but just not too much.
I pray about you,
and I'm not sure if it's enough.
I cry inside my soul,
my body has left me without any control.
I thought you were the same.
But when I talk to you, I can tell that things have
changed.
Please tell me, what did I do?
Was I just a fool?
Should I have known that this thing would not
pull through.
I want to know, I want to hear it from you.
I still love you.
Your my friend.
You're the one I'll always cherish until the very
end.
Beginning and starting again.
Let's do it all over and just be friends.

Longing Part 3

I'm afraid that you hurt me not once but twice.
So what is the difference of being here this time?
Beside me, close to me.
Too close to hurt me.
You have your ways,
You got your days.
You treat my feelings in ways I just can't
explain.
So while your out enjoying life, I'm struggling to
maintain.
It's like I feel your stare circulating through my
veins.
So what should I do now?
Should I just go on with life and try to forget
you somehow?
Should I go on and feel as if I'm without
the love, the feeling, the comfort of your touches
feeling?
Just focus on another's dealing,
as if from my heart you were stealing.
No I can't, that is not what I should do!
I can't, I wouldn't do it if you told me to!
Instead I'll settle down.
But I'll always remember who you were and
who you are.
And how this special space in my heart belongs
to you.

Thief In The Night

Just as a Thief in the night,
It came, I looked outside.
The color was a light greenish yellow.
This was the color of the sky.
"Wake up its time, the day of Jehovah is here!"
I look out the window, an Angel walks up and
leads us away.
"Listen carefully"
And walk behind
I look to the street a man curses God, all of a
sudden, he is gone.
Anticipation, satisfaction, relief.
Loving Jehovah paid off with my beliefs.
Strong conviction, always showing Jehovah his
deserved, honorable recognition.
Now we are prepared for everlasting blessings,
comfort and protection.
Nana, my Dad, everybody I love.
I see Briana, I see them in the resurrection.

Go With The Flow

I've been pondering,
So I guess that mentally I have been wandering.
Have I really thought about the pain that this
brings?
How you are deserving of blessings,
Your spiritual issues, are you addressing?
No more of the guns and killer knives.
Instead of murder we are trying to ave lives.
And when you let those hings in, anger leaves
your soul with hives.
If you don't shed tears, you cry inside.
If you don't like living, then you want to die.
You can't talk but expect me to read your mind.
Please let me know what it is you are trying to
hide.
Because we cant help you if we don't know how
you feel inside.
Does your heart feel like waves of an emotional
tide?
I don't know what to tell you
I don't know what to say
Just surf along and ride the waves.

Back to School Fair

17

So here we are at the "Back to School fair".
Cedric's the one that brought us
and I don't see him anywhere!

Irritated

I can't explain my fascination,
or even this disorderly emotional constipation.
Or even the way others perceive how I am when
I'm filled with irritation.
Your face somehow just causes aggravation.
I don't even admire the secrets of our relation.
Your the one who makes me sick,
and they make me vomit.
I'll scream and shout but still I can't stop it.
Anyways, I'm filled with joy! :)
I'm redundant in this faze, not even thinking
about pastor troy.
That girl over there is faster than that boy!
So who's power of understanding are you trying
to employ?

Hopeful

This sound that I make is that of a joyful cry.
My tears of happiness come from the most high.
When I look up, I realize that blessings come
from the sky.
From Jehovah, "The Most High"
Fear inspiring,
my love for him is untiring.
His love for me is admiring!
For look, the kings themselves have seen God's
glory in amazement.
Meeting together by appointment.
Oh, how they can't realize my blessing that are
heaven sent.
Their disturbance had them running in panic.
While they stare at me and how I've managed.
"Hear, you inhabitants of the earth"
Give ear to all who are not sure of what it's
worth.
This system of things is the founder of what
Satan brings.
And you wonder why praise to Jehovah is what I
sing.
You sons of mankind are sons of Man.
You rich ones couldn't, even if you tried to make
the poor stand.

So while Babylon is falling religion is what they
ban.
So, do you now?
Tell me if you understand.
Why should I be afraid in the days of evil,
when for yourselves you cause the great
upheaval?
Those who boast.. You who rely on your own
way of maintenance,
Watch how we rely on Jehovah in patience!

A Worthy Price

So what about your abundance of riches?
And the hearts you broke that you tried to mend
with stitches?
Show me where the love is.
And for you, the ones you hurt, tell me where
the trust is.
You're not worthy,
Your mind is dirty.
You kill others just because your hurting.
Can those whom you hurt, by any means redeem
themselves?
Not that you can or would even give to God a
ransom for the sake of him.
The redemption price is precious,
That it has ceased to time indefinite.

Endure

Jehovah is the only one who truly knows me.
Jehovah is the one who truly shows me.
Whenever I call Jehovah holds me.
And through Christ Jesus's example of love he
molds me.
In the heart of the vast seas the mountains have
tottered.
Through the dry deserted plains,
the sun has left the ground unwatered.
Through Christ Jesus our lord freedom rings.
Tell me, do you still believe that Dr. King had a
dream?
It was from the WORD, The published thought,
Love that God has shown us,
through the things his son has taught.
Example of life.
Enduring through strife.
Thank you Jehovah for making things right

Love Me Anyway

I'm thinking of how things used to be.
How it was when it was you and me.
You know that I love you still.
The thought of me not seeing you again gives
me chills.
Knowing that when I do ill be filled with thrills..
As I grow older into my teenage years,
I learn to love you way beyond my fears.
But my fears aren't of you, you brighten up my
day.
You give me the courage to go on in your own
special way.
My words are getting short, for now there is no
more to say.
Just that no matter what happens, I now you'll
love me anyway.

Dream for a Change

24

It was at a school & the wind was strong.
I had lied so much that I couldn't see the wrong.
I didn't tell the truth
I noticed as the tornado swept through.
I had this long.
I've hurt people.
I ruined lives,
but I prayed and I apologized.
I asked Jehovah for forgiveness.
And this tornado would've swept me away if I
hadn't become a Witness.